Anger

by Charles R. Swindoll

ZondervanPublishingHouse
Grand Rapids, Michigan

A Division of HarperCollins*Publishers*

Anger: The Burning Fuse of Hostility
© 1980, 1995 by Charles R. Swindoll, Inc.

Requests for information should be addressed to:
Zondervan Publishing House
5300 Patterson Avenue S.E.
Grand Rapids, Michigan 49530

ISBN 0-310-20070-9

The material in this booklet originally appeared in the book *Three Steps Forward, Two Steps Back* published by Thomas Nelson Publishers, Nashville, Tennessee.

Unless otherwise identified, all Scripture references are from the New American Standard Bible, © The Lockman Foundation 1960, 1962, 1963, 1968, 1971, 1972, 1973, 1975, 1977. Used by permission.

Verses taken from *The Amplified New Testament* © The Lockman Foundation 1954, 1958 are used by permission.

Verses marked NEB are from *The New English Bible* © The Delegates of the Oxford University Press and the Syndics of the Cambridge University Press 1961, 1970. Used by permission.

Verses marked MLB are from *The Modern Language Bible, The New Berkeley Version,* © 1959 © 1969 by Zondervan Publishing House. Used by permission.

All rights reserved. No part of this publication may be reproduced, stored in a retrieval system, or transmitted in any form—electronic, mechanical, photocopy, recording, or any other—without the prior permission of the publisher.

Printed in the United States of America

Cover Design by DesignTeam, Brian L. Fowler

95 96 97 98 00 / ❖ DP / 5 4 3 2 1

Introduction

From mild irritation to uncontrolled rage, anger wears many faces and plays numerous roles in our life. Sometimes justified, often not, anger is one of our emotions that must be kept under the dominating control of the Holy Spirit. Like fire, it can either be of benefit or cause permanent damage. Something *that* powerful deserves our full attention. And God's full control.

This booklet is dedicated to helping victims of anger get a grip on the problem. Without condemning, it offers straight-from-the-Scripture counsel that is sure to help. And best of all, it holds out hope to those who have struggled for years with an internal burning fuse of hostility.

- Do you need encouragement and assistance?
- Are you tired of losing the war with wrath?
- Have you been more irritated in recent days?
- Is your initial reaction to opposition a clenched fist?
- Would you rather fight than switch?

If so, these pages contain information that is essential to your spiritual survival.

You *can* know victory in the hot arena of everyday demands, difficult people, and irritating circumstances. Through God's help, a new beginning can start today!

Charles R. Swindoll

Anger

A great American statesman, Thomas Jefferson, worked out a way to handle his anger. He included it in his "Rules of Living," which describes how he believed adult men and women should live. He wrote this:

> When angry, count ten before you speak;
> If very angry, a hundred.[1]

Author Mark Twain, about seventy-five years later, revised Jefferson's words. He wrote:

> When angry, count four. When very angry, swear.[2]

I don't know of anything more frustrating to deal with than anger (it makes me mad!). It has a way of disarming us, of robbing us of our testimonies. It injures our home lives and our relationships with co-workers.

Some time ago a man sat in my study and poured out his anguish. He had battered his wife the night before. She was too humiliated (and bruised) to come with him. Both, by the way, are Christians.

I sat in the Orange County jail with a young father, his face buried in his hands. Tears ran through his fingers as he told me of his temper. He had just killed his infant daughter with his own hands—in an uncontrollable rage. He had been irritated by the baby's crying as he was listening to music.

No, anger isn't a humorous matter. It's something that must be understood, admitted, and kept under control, or it will literally slay us.

WHAT IS ANGER?

Let me begin by defining what anger is, and that's not easy. I've woven together several different resources and have come up with this definition:

> Anger is an emotional reaction of hostility that brings personal displeasure, either to ourselves or to someone else.

People who study psychology tell us that there are various phases of anger. All of us have experienced some of them.

Anger can begin with *mild irritation*, which is nothing more than perhaps an innocent experience of being upset, a mild feeling of discomfort brought about by someone or something.

Then anger can turn from irritation to *indignation,* which is a feeling that something must be answered; there must be an avenging of that which is wrong. But both irritation and indignation can go unexpressed.

If fed, indignation leads to *wrath*—which *never* goes unexpressed. Psychologists tell us that wrath is a strong desire to avenge.

Then, as it increases, anger becomes *fury.* The word suggests violence, even a loss of emotional control.

The last phase of anger is *rage.* Obviously, rage is the most dangerous form of anger.

In Los Angeles some time back, a man drowned his children—four of them. He admitted it happened in a fit of rage. Rage is a temporary loss of control involving acts of violence; the angry person scarcely realizes what he has done.

THE SCRIPTURES MAY SURPRISE YOU!

In Ephesians 4:26–27 we have two verses that have to do with anger.

> Be angry, and yet do not sin; do not let the sun go down on your anger, and do not give the devil an opportunity.

The Amplified Bible renders those verses this way:

> When angry, do not sin; do not ever let your wrath—your exasperation, your fury or indignation—last until the sun goes down. Leave no [such] room or foothold for the devil—give no opportunity to him.

The New English Bible says it this way:

> If you are angry, do not let anger lead you into sin; do not let sunset find you still nursing it; leave no loop-hole for the devil.

The very first time I looked at this verse in depth, I did a double-take. Do you realize that God is saying to you, "Get mad!" That's right. If that were the end of verse 26, we would put an exclamation point after the word "angry." Be angry! How about that! When's the last time you obeyed the Scriptures and "blew your cool"?

I see three important things in these verses. The first is simple and clear. *Anger is a God-given emotion.* There's something inhuman about a person who never gets angry. He has a strange makeup. We would be quick to say that one who does not show compassion really does not have a heart. And one who doesn't love—well, there's something terribly wrong with him. These emotions are God-given, and He says to express them. The same is true of anger. God says, "Be angry."

The second observation goes right along

with the first. *Anger is not necessarily sinful.* God says, "Be angry, and yet do not sin." Not every expression of anger is wrong. It's as though I were to say to one of my children, "Now, when you go out tonight, enjoy yourself. Really have a good time. But don't misuse your humor." Or it's like the Lord when He says, "I want you to love, but don't love the world. Don't even love the things of the world. I want you to love, but restrict that love to certain things." This is the same thought. Be angry, but don't carry that anger to the point where it becomes sin.

Some of you may be questioning whether or not it is *ever* right to be angry. Did you know that in the Old Testament "the anger of the Lord" is mentioned no less than eighteen times?

And in the New Testament we have some classic examples of Jesus' anger! When those moneychangers were in the temple, He didn't walk in and say, "Now listen, guys, I don't want to offend you, but what you are doing isn't very good." Rather, he plaited together a whip of thongs and physically drove them out of the temple. His was an expression of real indignation. He got mad!

And Jesus never spoke more angrily and forthrightly to anyone than He did to the religious hypocrites in Matthew 23, where in one case after another He said, "Woe to you." He even called them "whitewashed tombs" and "serpents"! There are times when anger is very appropriate. I'll say more about that later.

Third, *anger must have safeguards*. Notice the two safeguards Paul gave us right in this passage?

Safeguard number one:

> Do not let the sun go down on your anger (Ephesians 4:26).

Don't prolong anger into the night. In Paul's day, the setting of the sun was the closing of the day and the beginning of the next. By the end of the day, make sure your anger problem is solved.

I believe this is to be taken very literally. We practice this in our home; perhaps you do in yours. If there have been times of disagreement or anger throughout the day, clear them up by evening. When you lay your head on your pillow, make sure those feelings of anger have been resolved. Be certain that there is forgiveness, a clearing out of that conscience. Husbands and wives, don't go to sleep back to back. Don't allow yourself the luxury of feeling you can take care of it later on.

Every once in a while, a Christian brother or sister tells me of an experience when they flew off the handle. They were in the wrong. And they will say something like, "You know, as I turned in that night, things just didn't settle right." Maybe you've had that experience. I certainly have. Then they say, "I had to get up, turn the light on, and make a phone call ... or get dressed, go over to this person's house, and talk with him face to face to clear it up." It's a real encouragement to hear things like that.

Safeguard number two:

> Do not give the devil an opportunity (Ephesians 4:27).

That means just what it says. Don't allow your anger to be expressed in such a way that you are weakened and the devil reproduces his character through you.

You see, Jesus Christ loves to reproduce His character through us. When we are under the control of the Holy Spirit, then the character of Christ flows freely—His love, His gentleness, His compassion, His joy, His concern for others. But the devil is a master of counterfeit, and when we are given over to the things of Satan, he aims to make us behave like him.

That's Paul's whole point. Don't let anger get hold of you and weaken you so that other areas of sin, or even satanic involvement, can come into your life. Keep that in mind if you are prone to get angry. Sustained, uncontrolled anger offers the enemy of our souls an open door. It's serious.

WHEN IS ANGER JUSTIFIED?

When can we actually say it is right to

be angry? That's an important question. I find there are three specific situations in Scripture when anger is justifiable.

1. *When God's Word and God's will are knowingly disobeyed by God's people.* Something should happen in the heart of the child of God who sees other believers sinning openly, ignoring and disobeying the will of God. It's not good for us to look on passively. Something's wrong! When Moses saw what was going on around that golden calf, he couldn't handle it. He got downright indignant (see Exodus 32:19–20).

Further, there is an instance in Solomon's life that shows us the Lord does not overlook acts of carnality. First Kings 11 is the very tale of Solomon's last years. He had been blessed with riches, the likes of which the world has never known. The late J. Paul Getty would look like a bum compared to Solomon. He was loaded. And he had more wives and concubines, it seems, than any other man who has ever lived. He had more wisdom than anyone else in Scripture. But look at the latter part of his life.

> Now King Solomon loved many foreign women along with the daughter of Pharaoh: Moabite, Ammonite, Edomite, Sidonian, and Hittite women, from the nations concerning which the LORD had said to the sons of Israel, "You shall not associate with them, neither shall they

associate with you, for they will surely turn your heart away after their gods." Solomon held fast to these in love.

> And he had seven hundred wives, princesses, and three hundred concubines, and his wives turned his heart away. For it came about when Solomon was old, his wives turned his heart away after other gods; and his heart was not wholly devoted to the LORD his God, as the heart of David his father had been (1 Kings 11:1–4).

The next four verses describe his idolatrous practices. Then we read:

> Now the LORD was angry with Solomon because his heart was turned away from the LORD, the God of Israel, who had appeared to him twice, and had commanded him concerning this thing, that he should not go after other gods; but he did not observe what the LORD had commanded (1 Kings 11:9–10).

Anger is justified not only on man's part, but on the Lord's part when we openly and knowingly disobey His Word. On some fronts, grace has been twisted to convey the idea that God no longer has any standards, or that a godly quality of life is not expected of us, now that we're under grace. That is a perversion and a lie right out of the pit of hell!

There are other occasions in the Bible in which anger is justified.

2. *When God's enemies assume positions of jurisdiction outside their rights.* The prophet Isaiah records an example of the Lord's enemies moving into a realm outside their rights. The Lord rebuked them for it.

> Woe to those who call evil good, and good evil;
> Who substitute darkness for light and light for darkness....
> Woe to those who are wise in their own eyes,
> And clever in their own sight!
> Woe to those who are heroes in drinking wine,
> And valiant men in mixing strong drink;
> Who justify the wicked for a bribe [and now here's the phrase],
> And take away the rights of the ones who are in the right! [Woe to them!]
> Therefore, as a tongue of fire consumes stubble ...
> So their root will become like rot and their blossom blow away as dust;
> For they have rejected the law of the LORD of hosts,
> And despised the word of the Holy One of Israel.
> On this account the anger of the LORD has burned against His people (Isaiah 5:20–25).

The little phrase in verse 23 attracts my attention. "Those who take away the rights of the ones who are in the right!" My point is this: Anger is justified when enemies of the

Lord take away rights outside their realm of jurisdiction. Several examples could be shown from Scripture.

For example, in 1 Samuel 11, Saul is the anointed king when the enemy comes to invade the land. We read in 1 Samuel 11:6 that *"the Spirit of God came upon Saul mightily when he heard these words, and he became very angry."* Literally, his anger became intense, because war was being declared against the land of God and the people of Israel. Their freedom was being threatened.

I think this is very applicable for our day and our view of war. I can assure you that I am not a warmonger. No one hurts more than I do to see the results of war. No doubt, you feel the same. But this is not to say that when an enemy desires to come in and remove the freedom of our land that we should sit passively by and say, "Well, we just had better live with it. It's just one of those problems of life. Evil is on the earth." The Scriptures declare that when people take away the rights of those who are in the right, the Lord becomes angry ... and so should we. Defending these treasured rights is our responsibility.

3. A third situation where anger is justified is in Ephesians 6. It is *when children are dealt with unfairly by parents*. Here, we are no longer dealing with theory or some distant war or some court of law. We are now talk-

ing about justified anger in the home. I want to be very careful how I express myself, so that I won't be misunderstood.

> Children, obey your parents in the Lord, for this is right. Honor your father and mother (which is the first commandment with a promise), that it may be well with you, and that you may live long on the earth. And, fathers, do not provoke your children to anger; but bring them up in the discipline and instruction of the Lord (Ephesians 6:1–4).

The parallel verse in Colossians is:

> Fathers, do not exasperate your children, that they may not lose heart (Colossians 3:21).

It is interesting that in both passages, the apostle Paul specifically addressed *fathers*. We fathers often are given to impatience; to a lack of real understanding of the feelings of our little ones, our teenagers, or our young adults still living at home. When we exasperate our children by dealing with them unfairly and they respond in anger, this anger is justified. Do not provoke your children to anger!

And children, be careful that you do not look upon every word from your father's lips as provoking you to anger. I'm talking about those things fathers do that really bring about feelings of unfair hurt and irritation.

I want to say something that might be misunderstood, but I am still going to say it. I think some of us are twisting the teaching of the "chain of command" in the home way beyond its proper bounds. Anyone can take a good truth and pervert it, and I know of cases where this has been done.

Be careful as a husband, a father, a man of God, that your dealings with your family are *fair* and that you can, before God, support them scripturally and logically. Be sensitive to your wife and children. Don't use the concept of the "chain of command" as a brutal, bloody club, lording it over your family. Instead, be an authority that *serves*. (This topic is discussed at length in two of my books, *You and Your Child* and *Improving Your Serve*.)

Are you given to unjustified anger? Have doors been slammed closed in your home or with your friends simply because you lost your temper? Ephesians 4:31–32 reads:

> Let all bitterness and wrath and anger and clamor and slander be put away from you, along with all malice. And be kind to one another, tenderhearted, forgiving each other, just as God in Christ also has forgiven you.

The wrath of God was poured out on Jesus Christ at Calvary. All His anger at sin was, at that point in time, poured out on the

Savior. He knows what anger is like; you can pour yours out upon Him. He wants to take that weakness, that area of sin, and give you victory in it.

UNJUSTIFIED ANGER

Let's dig deeper. We can't leave the subject until we look at the other side of the coin. When is anger unjustified?

1. *When anger comes from the wrong motive.* We've all studied the prodigal son, but we usually miss the prodigal that stayed home! He is the one who illustrates an anger that was not justified because it sprang from a wrong motive. When the younger brother came to himself, he was, you will recall, in a swine pen. He was at the end of his rope, and the Scripture says:

> But when he came to his senses, he said, "... I will get up and go to my father, and will say to him, 'I am no longer worthy to be called your son; make me as one of your hired men'" (Luke 15:17–19).

And he did that. You know the rest of the story. The father greeted him with open arms, delighted to have him there. But this joy was not shared by the wayward son's older brother.

> Now his older son was in the field, and when he came and approached the house, he heard music and dancing. And he summoned one of the servants and

began inquiring what these things might be. And he said to him, "Your brother has come, and your father has killed the fattened calf, because he has received him back safe and sound" (Luke 15:25–27).

Now notice the *jealous motive* that resulted in anger.

> But he became angry, and was not willing to go in; and his father came out and began entreating him. But he answered and said to his father, "Look! For so many years I have been serving you, and I have never neglected a command of yours; and yet you have never given me a kid, that I might be merry with my friends; but when this son of yours came [notice he doesn't call him "my brother"; he was tremendously angry], who has devoured your wealth with harlots [How does he know that? The Bible never tells us his brother visited prostitutes. It's possible, but when you're angry and jealous, you exaggerate the story.], you killed the fattened calf for him."
>
> And he [the father] said to him, "My child, you have always been with me, and all that is mine is yours. But we had to be merry and rejoice, for this brother of yours was dead and has begun to live, and was lost and has been found" (Luke 15:28–32).

When we are jealous of some other person, our response is frequently one of anger, especially when that other person receives some kind of commendation or promotion or attention from other people. "It isn't fair! That's my right to enjoy, not his!" That anger is unjustified.

The thing we must ask ourselves when anger begins to come is, "What is the motive behind my feelings?"

2. *When things don't go your way.* The Book of Jonah contains the most extensive revival recorded in history. The entire city of Nineveh—believed by many Old Testament scholars to be half a million or more in population—repented of their sins and turned to the Lord.

Jonah, of course, was a bigoted racist. He was a prophet, indeed, but he was a man who really wanted to see Nineveh destroyed, something of an ancient Archie Bunker! That is why he didn't go to Nineveh when God told him to the first time. He did not want Nineveh to repent; he wanted it blasted away. And he got angry because things didn't go his way.

> When God saw their deeds, that they turned from their wicked way, then God relented concerning the calamity which He had declared He would bring upon them. And He did not do it. But it greatly displeased Jonah, and he became angry (Jonah 3:10–4:1).

Notice that the reason for his anger was that

he didn't get his way—he wanted destruction, but God gave deliverance.

> And he prayed to the LORD and said, "Please LORD, was not this what I said while I was still in my own country? ["This is why I didn't want to go in the first place."] ... Therefore now, O LORD, please take my life from me, for death is better to me than life."
>
> And the LORD said, "Do you have good reason to be angry?" (Jonah 4:2–4).

Jonah went out to a hillside, refusing to answer the Lord. He sat down under a nice, leafy gourd vine to enjoy a little shade. Sitting comfortably there on that hill, the wind blowing softly, he thought, "My, this is living." Here, he could quickly forget about Nineveh. Then a little worm came and ate up that gourd plant, and it wilted. Jonah got hot and bothered, and begged God to take his life.

> Then God said to Jonah, "Do you have good reason to be angry about the plant?" (Jonah 4:9).

This brings us to a very practical point: We really do like to have our own way. For example, you work hard all week and you think, "I will have a nice evening out with my wife on Friday night." You get it all arranged, and you drive to your favorite restaurant. There's a long line, but you are not worried. You walk up to the front and say, "I called in reservations for tonight."

The hostess says, "I'm sorry, sir, but I don't have your name written down here."

How do you respond? Unless I miss my guess, you become angry. Rather than saying, "Lord, what can I learn through this?" you think, "Listen, I've got my rights!"

"But I called in two days ago," you protest.

"Sorry."

So you wait in line. Steaming. Frowning. When you finally are seated, you get a bad table (it's near the door and the legs are uneven) and your waitress is irritable. Your food is cold. The candle goes out. The people around you are loud and boisterous.

This is where Christianity is put on the block. The real test is not in a Sunday service. It's in a Friday night restaurant when things don't go our way.

One of the best ways I know to keep from getting angry when we don't get our way is to have a good sense of humor. Turn the bad times into a little fun.

When we were living in Texas, our family planned for months to go to a state park for a camping vacation. We looked forward to it, but before we left we prayed, "Lord, whatever happens, we're going to have a good time."

It was a good thing we prayed that,

because the place was a rat-hole. There were wall-to-wall people. It was hot—the weather was terrible! It was a great disappointment. We spent one night with spiders and scorpions, laughed it off, and headed back home. On the way, we stopped off at another state park where there wasn't a soul. I still can't understand it. We checked in and spent almost two full weeks in a place that was marvelously quiet and delightful, unseasonably cool and picturesque.

God seems to reward us with good, delightful experiences when we move with joy through those times when we didn't get our own way. The choice is ours. If we choose to be offended when we don't get our own way, then we're going to live constantly on the edge of anger. But if we say to ourselves, "A merry heart does good like a medicine," it'll make all the difference in the world.

3. *When you react too quickly without investigating the facts.*

> The end of a matter is better than its beginning; Patience of spirit is better than haughtiness of spirit. Do not be eager in your heart to be angry, For anger resides in the bosom of fools (Ecclesiastes 7:8–9).

> But let everyone be quick to hear, slow to speak and slow to anger (James 1:19).

If we have a *patient* spirit, if we *hear a matter out*, it is better than just hearing its beginning. If we are eager in our hearts to be angry, we're foolish.

It's a real concern to me that we have to live at such a hurried, harried pace. When the schedule is not met, the instant response of the foolish one is anger. Retaliate. Fight back. The writer of Ecclesiastes is saying, "If you do that, you're a fool."

This struck me during a past family vacation. It was amazing how much more patient we were when we got some times of sustained quietness. We were camping deep in the heart of the giant redwoods up near the Oregon border. Beneath the glow of our little red Coleman lantern, we sat around a fire each night. Quietness was all around. Each morning we arose to the chirp of birds and the river's rippling rapids. I don't think we'll ever forget it! As I recall, we didn't have one bout with anger during the whole three weeks.

Develop the art of quietness. Turn off the appliances, including the TV. In fact, wean yourself from it for an entire evening. Leave it off. Honestly, we will never become men and women of God without experiencing some solitude.

WINNING OVER ANGER

What do we do about anger? *When it comes from a wrong motive, when we don't get our own way, when we act in haste*—anger is sin. What practical things does God say about dealing with anger? Scripture offers four specific directives in the book of Proverbs. Let's cover them quickly.

1. *Learn to ignore petty disagreements.*

> A man's discretion makes him slow to anger,
> And it is his glory to overlook a transgression (Proverbs 19:11).

Perhaps it is better rendered in the Berkeley Version.

> It is prudent for a man to restrain his anger; it is his glory to overlook an offense (MLB).

In God's eyes, it is *glory* if you are big enough to overlook an offense. Don't look for a fight, Christian. Keep the chip off your shoulder. Don't be defensive about your point or your right. Be willing to give.

Proverbs 17:14 says essentially the same thing. I like this verse.

> The beginning of strife is like letting out water,
> So abandon the quarrel before it breaks out.

Just as in the tango, it takes two to quarrel. If you see that there is an angry disagreement coming, back off; leave it. Learn to ignore petty differences.

2. *Refrain from close association with anger-prone people.* Don't hang around them.

> Do not associate with a man given to anger;
> Or go with a hot-tempered man,
> Lest you learn his ways,
> And find a snare for yourself (Proverbs 22:24–25).

It's true: We become like those we spend our time with. If you spend time with a rebel you will become rebellious and angry. If I hang around people who are negative, you know what happens to me? I become negative. (And by nature, I'm a positive person.) But it's amazing—the more I'm around people who talk about how things won't work, and how this isn't good, and how even though there were ten very fine things, two things went wrong, the more I begin to think, "You know, a lot of things are wrong." Then I get petty and negative in other areas.

Are you becoming an angry person because you're associating closely with angry people? The Scripture says, "Don't do it!"

3. *Keep very close check on your tongue.* More than any slanderous event, any immoral act, any unwise financial dealings, that which breaks up a church quickest is an unchecked tongue. The longer I live, the more I realize that.

> A gentle answer turns away wrath,
> But a harsh word stirs up anger
> (Proverbs 15:1).

Washington Irving made this statement:

> The only edged tool that gets sharper with use is the tongue.[3]

It isn't your leg muscle that's the strongest muscle in your body; it's the muscle in your mouth. Control your tongue. It will literally "turn away wrath."

4. *Cultivate honesty in communication ... don't let anger build up.* Take a close look at Proverbs 27:4–6:

> Wrath is fierce and anger is a flood,
> But who can stand before jealousy?
> Better is open rebuke
> Than love that is concealed.
> Faithful are the wounds of a friend,
> But deceitful are the kisses of an enemy.

The New Testament counterpart to this passage is Ephesians 4:25:

> Therefore, laying aside falsehood, speak truth, each one of you, with his neighbor, for we are members of one another.

There is no substitute for total honesty, spoken in love. Allowing anger to seethe on the back burner will lead to a very large lid blowing off a very hot pot. Let me encourage you to pick up a copy of David Augsburger's fine book, *Caring Enough to Con-*

front.[4] In that little volume you'll find an excellent treatment of this whole subject. Augsburger offers some outstanding guidelines on how to communicate honestly, yet lovingly.

Well, you've done enough thinking about anger. Enough of theory! Now it's time to put it into action. Not like Mark Twain suggested, or even like Thomas Jefferson ... but like the Bible directs.

> Lord of our lives:
> The old hymn speaks the truth of our hearts:
> "I need Thee every hour ..."
> The temptation to get mad is an "every hour" assault. We are so weary of the battle! And yet each new day introduces another set of irritations that bring the caldron of our souls to a slow boil. It isn't long before our thoughts and tongues spill over with bursts of anger ... sometimes so strong it frightens us. And fractures our relationship with others.
> We come to You with a simple yet sincere request. Nothing elaborate. No bargaining, no hidden motive. Just a direct, specific, one-word prayer to You, our only hope.
> "Help!"
> Help us with circumstances that corner us. Help us with people who aggravate us. Help us handle comments that stab and sting. Help us to have enough discernment to be angry about the right

things and yet enough control to hold it in check when we should.

Help, Lord. We need You *every* hour. It is in the all-powerful name of Your Son we pray.

Amen.

---

[1] Thomas Jefferson, *A Decalogue of Canons for Observation in Practical Life* (February 21, 1825), reprinted in *Familiar Quotations*, John Bartlett, ed., 376.

[2] Twain, *Pudd'nhead Wilson's Calendar*, Ch. 3, *Familiar Quotations*, John Bartlett, ed., 678.

[3] Washington Irving, *The Sketch-Book* (1819–1820), reprinted in *Familiar Quotations*, John Bartlett, ed., 446.

[4] David Augsburger, *Caring Enough to Confront* (Glendale, Calif.: Regal Books, 1973).

Other Booklets by Chuck Swindoll:

Attitudes

Commitment

Dealing with Defiance

Demonism

Destiny

Divorce

Eternal Security

Fun is Contagious

God's Will

Hope

Impossibilities

Integrity

Leisure

The Lonely Whine of the Top Dog

Moral Purity

Our Mediator

Peace ... in Spite of Panic

The Power of a Promise

Prayer

Sensuality

Singleness

Stress

This is No Time for Wimps!

Tongues

When Your Comfort Zone Gets the Squeeze

Woman